BE

STILL

...and know that I am God.

PSALM 46:10

The Lord Almighty is with us; the God of Jacob is our fortress. Come and see what the Lord has done, the desolations he has brought on the earth. He makes wars cease to the ends of the earth. He breaks the bow and shatters the spear; he burns the shields with fire. He says, "Be still, and know that I am God; I will be exalted among the nations, I will be exalted in the earth." The Lord Almighty is with us; the God of Jacob is our fortress. PSALM 46:7-11

TO:

_____

FROM:

_____

DATE:

_____

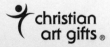

The LORD is my *light* and my *salvation*. Ps. 27:1

"All things are *possible* with God." Mark 10:27

I can do all this through Him who gives me *strength*. PHIL. 4:13

Mercy, peace and *love* be yours in abundance. JUDE 1:2

"Be *still*, and know that I am God." Ps. 46:10

Every good and *perfect* gift is from above. JAMES 1:17

"Where your *treasure* is, there your *heart* will be also." Matt. 6:21

If anything is *excellent or praiseworthy—think* about such things. Phil. 4:8

God...does great things *beyond* our *understanding*. Job 37:5

Give *thanks* to the LORD, for He is good; His *love* endures *forever*. Ps. 118:29

Trust in the LORD with all your heart. PROV. 3:5

I will *sing* the LORD's *praise*, for He has been good to me. Ps. 13:6

Great are the *works* of the Lord. Ps. 111:2

The Lord will *guide* you always. Isa. 58:11

"I am the *way* and the *truth* and the *life*." JOHN 14:6

Be *joyful* in hope, *patient* in affliction, *faithful* in prayer. Rom. 12:12

"*Rejoice* and be glad, because great is your reward in *heaven*." MATT. 5:12

"*Everything* is possible for one who *believes*." MARK 9:23

Let us *love* one another, for love comes from God. 1 John 4:7

Let the *peace* of Christ rule in your *hearts*. COL. 3:15

The LORD is *near* ... to all who call on Him in *truth*. Ps. 145:18

Truly my soul finds *rest* in God. Ps. 62:1

The Lord your God will *bless* you...in all the work of your *hands*. Deut. 16:15

"My *Presence* will go with you, and I will give you *rest*." Exod. 33:14

Cast all your anxiety on Him because He *cares* for you. 1 PET. 5:7

"Your Father *knows* what you need *before* you ask Him." Matt. 6:8

The LORD is my *shepherd*, I lack *nothing*. Ps. 23:1

"*Peace* I leave with you; My peace I *give* you." John 14:27

My times are in *Your hands*. Ps. 31:15

The *plans* of the LORD stand firm *forever*. Ps. 33:11

The LORD gives *wisdom*; from His mouth come *knowledge* and *understanding*. PROV. 2:6

If...you *seek* the Lord your God, you will *find* Him. Deut. 4:29

The LORD is my *light* and my *salvation*. Ps. 27:1

"All things are *possible* with God." MARK 10:27

I can do all this through Him who gives me *strength*. Phil. 4:13

Mercy, peace and *love* be yours in abundance. JUDE 1:2

"Be *still*, and know that I am God." Ps. 46:10

Every good and *perfect* gift is from above. JAMES 1:17

"Where your *treasure* is, there your *heart* will be also." MATT. 6:21

If anything is *excellent or praiseworthy—think* about such things. PHIL. 4:8

God...does great things *beyond* our *understanding*. JOB 37:5

Give *thanks* to the LORD, for He is good; His *love* endures *forever*. Ps. 118:29

Trust in the LORD with all your heart. PROV. 3:5

I will *sing* the LORD's *praise*, for He has been good to me. Ps. 13:6

Great are the *works* of the LORD. Ps. 111:2

The LORD will *guide* you always. Isa. 58:11

"I am the *way* and the *truth* and the *life*." JOHN 14:6

Be *joyful* in hope, *patient* in affliction, *faithful* in prayer. ROM. 12:12

"Rejoice and be glad, because great is your reward in *heaven."* MATT. 5:12

"*Everything* is possible for one who *believes*." MARK 9:23

Let us *love* one another, for love comes from God. 1 JOHN 4:7

Let the *peace* of Christ rule in your *hearts*. COL. 3:15

The Lord is *near* ... to all who call on Him in *truth*. Ps. 145:18

Truly my soul finds *rest* in God. Ps. 62:1

The LORD your God will *bless* you...in all the work of your *hands*. DEUT. 16:15

"My *Presence* will go with you, and I will give you *rest*." EXOD. 33:14

Cast all your anxiety on Him because He *cares* for you. 1 Pet. 5:7

"Your Father *knows* what you need *before* you ask Him." MATT. 6:8

The LORD is my *shepherd*, I lack *nothing*. Ps. 23:1

"*Peace* I leave with you; My peace I *give* you." JOHN 14:27

My times are in *Your hands.* Ps. 31:15

The *plans* of the Lᴏʀᴅ stand firm *forever*. Ps. 33:11

The Lord gives *wisdom*; from His mouth come *knowledge* and *understanding*. Prov. 2:6

If … you *seek* the LORD your God, you will *find* Him. DEUT. 4:29

The LORD is my *light* and my *salvation*. Ps. 27:1

"All things are *possible* with God." MARK 10:27

I can do all this through Him who gives me *strength*. PHIL. 4:13

Mercy, peace and *love* be yours in abundance. JUDE 1:2

"Be *still*, and know that I am God." Ps. 46:10

Every good and *perfect* gift is from above. JAMES 1:17

If anything is *excellent or praiseworthy* – *think* about such things. PHIL. 4:8

God...does great things *beyond* our *understanding.* JOB 37:5

Give *thanks* to the LORD, for He is good; His *love* endures *forever*. Ps. 118:29

Trust in the LORD with all your heart. PROV. 3:5

I will *sing* the LORD's *praise*, for He has been good to me. Ps. 13:6

Great are the _works_ of the LORD. Ps. 111:2

The LORD will *guide* you always. Isa. 58:11

"I am the *way* and the *truth* and the *life*." JOHN 14:6

Be *joyful* in hope, *patient* in affliction, *faithful* in prayer. Rom. 12:12

"*Rejoice* and be glad, because great is your reward in *heaven.*" Matt. 5:12

"*Everything* is possible for one who *believes*." MARK 9:23

Let us *love* one another, for love comes from God. 1 JOHN 4:7

Let the *peace* of Christ rule in your *hearts*. Col. 3:15

The LORD is *near* ... to all who call on Him in *truth*. Ps. 145:18

Truly my soul finds *rest* in God. Ps. 62:1

The LORD your God will *bless* you...in all the work of your *hands*. DEUT. 16:15

"My *Presence* will go with you, and I will give you *rest*." Exod. 33:14

Cast all your anxiety on Him because He *cares* for you. 1 Pet. 5:7

"Your Father *knows* what you need *before* you ask Him." MATT. 6:8

The LORD is my *shepherd*, I lack *nothing*. Ps. 23:1

"*Peace* I leave with you; My peace I *give* you." JOHN 14:27

My times are in *Your hands*. Ps. 31:15

The *plans* of the LORD stand firm *forever*. Ps. 33:11

The Lord gives *wisdom*; from His mouth come *knowledge* and *understanding*. PROV. 2:6

If…you *seek* the Lord your God, you will *find* Him. Deut. 4:29

The Lord is my *light* and my *salvation*. Ps. 27:1

"All things are *possible* with God." Mark 10:27

I can do all this through Him who gives me *strength*. PHIL. 4:13

Mercy, peace and *love* be yours in abundance. JUDE 1:2

"Be *still*, and know that I am God." Ps. 46:10

Every good and *perfect* gift is from above. JAMES 1:17

"Where your *treasure* is, there your *heart* will be also." Matt. 6:21

If anything is *excellent or praiseworthy—think* about such things. Phil. 4:8

God...does great things *beyond* our *understanding*. JOB 37:5

Give *thanks* to the LORD, for He is good; His *love* endures *forever*. Ps. 118:29

Trust in the LORD with all your heart. PROV. 3:5

I will *sing* the LORD's *praise*, for He has been good to me. Ps. 13:6

Great are the *works* of the LORD. Ps. 111:2

The LORD will *guide* you always. Isa. 58:11

"I am the *way* and the *truth* and the *life*." John 14:6

Be *joyful* in hope, *patient* in affliction, *faithful* in prayer. Rom. 12:12

"*Rejoice* and be glad, because great is your reward in *heaven*." Matt. 5:12

"*Everything* is possible for one who *believes*." MARK 9:23

Let us *love* one another, for love comes from God. 1 JOHN 4:7

Let the *peace* of Christ rule in your *hearts*. COL. 3:15

The Lord is *near* ... to all who call on Him in *truth*. Ps. 145:18

Truly my soul finds *rest* in God. Ps. 62:1

The LORD your God will *bless* you...in all the work of your *hands*. DEUT. 16:15

"My *Presence* will go with you, and I will give you *rest*." Exod. 33:14

Cast all your anxiety on Him because He *cares* for you. 1 Pet. 5:7

"Your Father *knows* what you need *before* you ask Him." Matt. 6:8

The Lord is my *shepherd*, I lack *nothing*. Ps. 23:1

"*Peace* I leave with you; My peace I *give* you." John 14:27

My times are in *Your hands*. Ps. 31:15

The *plans* of the LORD stand firm *forever*. Ps. 33:11

The LORD gives *wisdom*; from His mouth come *knowledge* and *understanding*. PROV. 2:6

If ... you *seek* the LORD your God, you will *find* Him. DEUT. 4:29

The Lord is my *light* and my *salvation*. Ps. 27:1

"All things are *possible* with God." MARK 10:27

I can do all this through Him who gives me *strength*. PHIL. 4:13

Mercy, peace and *love* be yours in abundance. JUDE 1:2

"Be *still*, and know that I am God." Ps. 46:10

Every good and *perfect* gift is from above. JAMES 1:17

"Where your *treasure* is, there your *heart* will be also." Matt. 6:21

If anything is *excellent or praiseworthy—think* about such things. PHIL. 4:8

God...does great things *beyond* our *understanding*. JOB 37:5

Give *thanks* to the LORD, for He is good; His *love* endures *forever*. Ps. 118:2

Trust in the LORD with all your heart. PROV. 3:5

I will *sing* the LORD'S *praise*, for He has been good to me. Ps. 13:6

Great are the *works* of the LORD. Ps. 111:2

The LORD will *guide* you always. Isa. 58:11

Be *joyful* in hope, *patient* in affliction, *faithful* in prayer. Rom. 12:12

"*Rejoice* and be glad, because great is your reward in *heaven*." MATT. 5:12

"*Everything* is possible for one who *believes.*" MARK 9:23

Let us *love* one another, for love comes from God. 1 John 4:7

Let the *peace* of Christ rule in your *hearts*. Col. 3:15

The LORD is *near* ... to all who call on Him in *truth*. Ps. 145:18

Truly my soul finds *rest* in God. Ps. 62:1

The LORD your God will *bless* you...in all the work of your *hands*. DEUT. 16:15

"My *Presence* will go with you, and I will give you *rest*." EXOD. 33:14

Cast all your anxiety on Him because He *cares* for you. 1 Pet. 5:7

"Your Father *knows* what you need *before* you ask Him." Matt. 6:8

The Lord is my *shepherd*, I lack *nothing*. Ps. 23:1

"*Peace* I leave with you; My peace I *give* you." JOHN 14:27

My times are in *Your hands.* Ps. 31:15

The *plans* of the Lord stand firm *forever*. Ps. 33:11

The LORD gives *wisdom*; from His mouth come *knowledge* and *understanding*. PROV. 2:6

If ... you *seek* the Lord your God, you will *find* Him. Deut. 4:29

The LORD is my *light* and my *salvation*. Ps. 27:1

"All things are *possible* with God." MARK 10:27

I can do all this through Him who gives me *strength*. Phil. 4:13

Mercy, peace and *love* be yours in abundance. JUDE 1:2

"Be *still*, and know that I am God." Ps. 46:10

Every good and *perfect* gift is from above. JAMES 1:17

"Where your *treasure* is, there your *heart* will be also." MATT. 6:21

If anything is *excellent or praiseworthy – think* about such things. Phil. 4:8

God...does great things *beyond* our *understanding*. JOB 37:5

Give *thanks* to the L<small>ORD</small>, for He is good; His *love* endures *forever*. Ps. 118:29

Trust in the LORD with all your heart. PROV. 3:5

I will *sing* the Lord's *praise*, for He has been good to me. Ps. 13:6

Great are the *works* of the LORD. Ps. 111:2

The LORD will *guide* you always. Isa. 58:11

"I am the *way* and the *truth* and the *life*." John 14:6

Be *joyful* in hope, *patient* in affliction, *faithful* in prayer. Rom. 12:12

"*Rejoice* and be glad, because great is your reward in *heaven*." MATT. 5:12

"*Everything* is possible for one who *believes*." MARK 9:23

Let us *love* one another, for love comes from God. 1 JOHN 4:7

Let the *peace* of Christ rule in your *hearts.* Col. 3:15

The Lord is *near* ... to all who call on Him in *truth*. Ps. 145:18

Truly my soul finds *rest* in God. Ps. 62:1

The LORD your God will *bless* you...in all the work of your *hands*. DEUT. 16:15

"My *Presence* will go with you, and I will give you *rest*." Exod. 33:14

Cast all your anxiety on Him because He *cares* for you. 1 Pet. 5:7

"Your Father *knows* what you need *before* you ask Him." Matt. 6:8

The LORD is my *shepherd*, I lack *nothing*. Ps. 23:1

"*Peace* I leave with you; My peace I *give* you." JOHN 14:27

My times are in *Your hands*. Ps. 31:15

The *plans* of the Lord stand firm *forever*. Ps. 33:11

BE
✦ STILL ✦

... and know that I am God.
PSALM 46:10